Piano · Vocal · Guitar

CHART HITS OF 1999→2000

CONTENTS

ISBN 0-634-01574-5

HAL·LEONARD®
CORPORATION
7777 W. BLUEMOUND RD. P.O. BOX 13819 MILWAUKEE, WI 53213

Visit Hal Leonard Online at
www.halleonard.com

AMAZED

Words and Music by MARV GREEN,
CHRIS LINDSEY and AIMEE MAYO

Moderately slow Country Ballad

with pedal

Ev - 'ry time our eyes meet, this feel - in' in - side me
The smell of your skin, the taste of your kiss,

is al - most more than I___ can take.___
the way you whis - per in___ the dark.___

*Recorded a half step lower.

ba-by, I'm a-mazed by you.

ba-by, I'm a-mazed by you.

Ev-'ry lit-tle thing that you do.

I'm so in love with you. It just keeps get-tin' bet - ter.

GENIE IN A BOTTLE

Words and Music by STEVE KIPNER,
DAVID FRANK and PAM SHEYNE

ANGEL

Words and Music by
SARAH McLACHLAN

Original key: Db major. This edition has been transposed down one half-step to be more playable.

GET IT ON TONITE

Words and Music by MONTELL JORDAN, JORG EVANS,
JURGEN KORDULETSCH, DARREN BENBOW,
ANTOINE WILSON and BRIAN PALMER

THE HARDEST THING

Words and Music by STEVE KIPNER
and DAVID FRANK

HEARTBREAKER

Words and Music by MARIAH CAREY, JAY-Z,
SHIRLEY ELLISTON, LINCOLN CHASE,
NARADA MICHAEL WALDEN and JEFFREY COHEN

game on __ me? I should have known right from the start you'd go __ and break my heart. __

Gim-me your love, gim-me your love, gim-me your love, gim-me your love,

gim-me your love, gim-me your love, gim-me your love, gim-me your love. It's a

did you have to run your game on __ me? I should have

Male, Spoken: I'm al - most read - y.

gim-me your love,   gim-me your love,   gim-me your love,   gim-me your love.

Rap Lyrics

She wanna shout with Jay, play box with Jay.
She wanna pillow fight in the middle of the night.
She wanna drive my Benz with five of her friends.
She wanna creep past the block, spying again.
She wanna roll with Jay, chase skeeos away.
She wanna fight with lame chicks, blow my day.
She wanna respect the rest, kick me to the curb
If she find one strand of hair longer than hers.

She want love in the jacuzzi, rub up in the movies,
Access to the old crib, keys to the new, please.
She wanna answer the phone, tattoo her arm.
That's when I gotta send her back to her mom.
She call me "heartbreaker." When we apart, it makes her
Want a piece of paper, scribble down "I hate ya."
But she knows she love Jay, because
She love everything Jay say, Jay does, and uh,...

I DRIVE MYSELF CRAZY

Words and Music by RICK NOWELS,
ELLEN SHIPLEY and ALAN RICH

Moderately slow

Oh ____ oh. ____ Ooh ____ ooh. ____

____ Ly-ing in your arms so close to-geth-er,
I was such a fool. I could-n't see it,

did-n't know just what I ____ had. ____
just how good you were to ____ me. ____

I NEED TO KNOW

Words and Music by CORY ROONEY
and MARC ANTHONY

Moderately, not too fast

They say a- round __ the way __ you've asked __

My ev- 'ry thought __ is of __ this be -

Original key: B♭ minor. This edition has been transposed down one half-step to be more playable.

I STILL BELIEVE

Words and Music by BEPPE CANTARELLI
and ANTONINA ARMATO

I TRY

Lyrics by MACY GRAY
Music by MACY GRAY, JEREMY RUZUMNA,
JINSOO LIM and DAVID WILDER

I WANNA LOVE YOU FOREVER

Words and Music by SAM WATTERS
and LOUIS BIANCANIELLO

You set my soul __ at ease, __ chased
My mind fails to un - der - stand __ what my

dark - ness out __ of view, _____ left your des - p'rate spell __ on me.
heart __ tells me __ to do. _____ And I'd give up all __ I have

I WILL REMEMBER YOU
Theme from THE BROTHERS McMULLEN

Words and Music by SARAH McLACHLAN,
SEAMUS EGAN and DAVE MERENDA

IF YOU HAD MY LOVE

Words and Music by RODNEY JERKINS,
LASHAWN DANIELS, CORY ROONEY,
FRED JERKINS and JENNIFER LOPEZ

Moderate steady beat

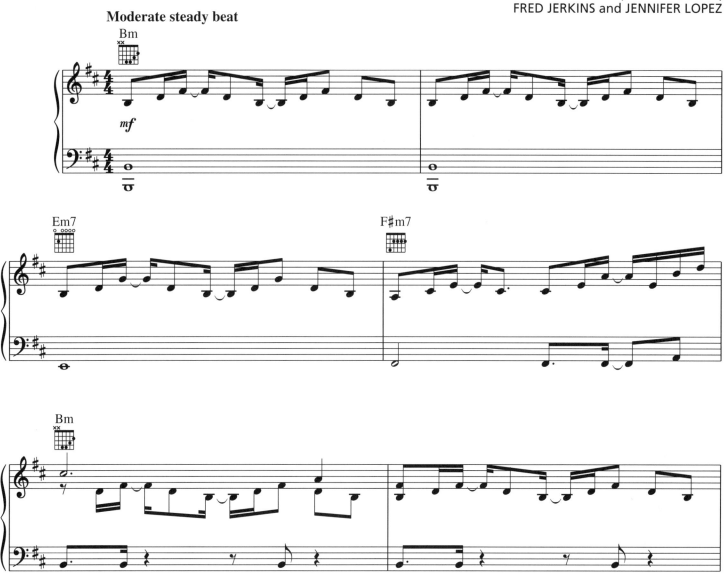

If ____

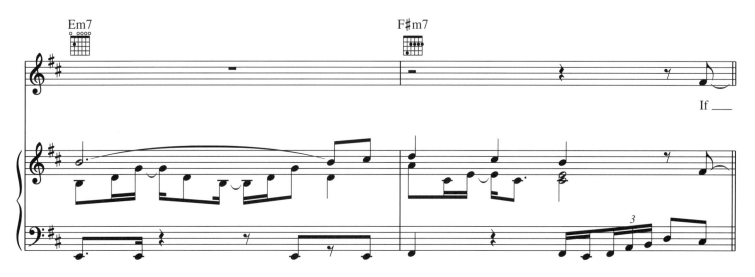

LAST KISS

Words and Music by
WAYNE COCHRAN

Oh where, oh where can my ___ ba - by be? ___

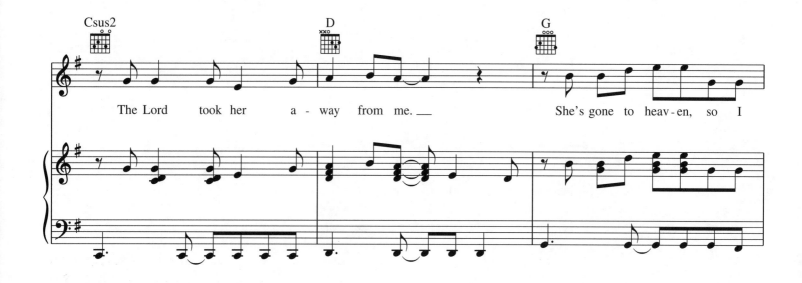

The Lord took her a - way from me. ___ She's gone to heav - en, so I

got to be good ___ so I can see my ba - by when I leave ___ this

LULLABY

Words and Music by
SHAWN MULLINS

Sonny and Cher.

I sing:

Ev - er - y - thing's _____ gon - na be all right. ____ Rock - a - bye, _

_ rock - a - bye. _____

CODA

rock - a - bye. _____

1. *(Spoken:) I told her I ain't so*
2. *Seems like*

sure about this place.
everybody's got a plan.

It's hard to
It's kind of like

MAMBO NO. 5
(A Little Bit Of...)

Original Music by DAMASO PEREZ PRADO
Words by LOU BEGA and ZIPPY

Relaxed two-beat feel

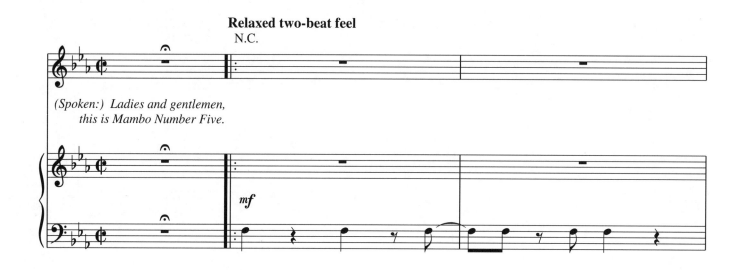

(Spoken:) Ladies and gentlemen, this is Mambo Number Five.

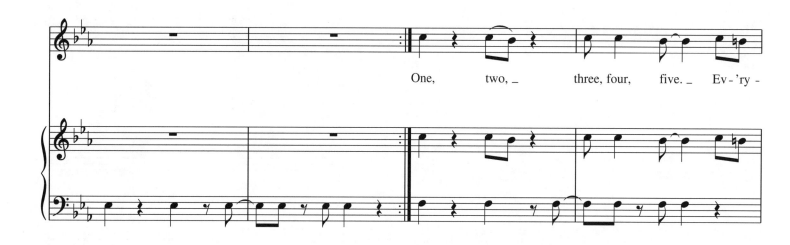

One, two, _ three, four, five. _ Ev-'ry-

bod-y in the car. So, come on, let's ride _ to the li-quor store a-round the

MARIA, MARIA

Words and Music by WYCLEF JEAN, JERRY DUPLESSIS,
CARLOS SANTANA, KARL PERAZZO and PAUL REKOW

MEET VIRGINIA

Words and Music by PAT MONAHAN,
JIMMY STAFFORD and ROB HOTCHKISS

SOMETIMES

Words and Music by
JORGEN ELOFSSON

MY LOVE IS YOUR LOVE

Words and Music by WYCLEF JEAN
and JERRY DUPLESSIS

NO SCRUBS

Words and Music by KANDI L. BURRUSS,
TAMEKA COTTLE and KEVIN BRIGGS

Original key: G♯ minor. This edition has been transposed down one half-step to be more playable.

TEARIN' UP MY HEART

Words and Music by MAX MARTIN
and KRISTIAN LUNDIN

UNPRETTY

Words and Music by DALLAS AUSTIN
and TIONNE WATKINS

*Vocal line is written an octave higher than sung.

Lyrics:

I wish I could tie you up __ in my __ shoes, __ make you feel un-pret-ty, too.

Nev-er in-se-cure un-til __ I met __ you. __ Now I'm be-in' stu-pid.

Vocal line is written as sung.

THANK GOD I FOUND YOU

Words and Music by MARIAH CAREY,
JAMES HARRIS III and TERRY LEWIS

*Vocal line is written one octave higher than sung.

(YOU DRIVE ME) CRAZY

Words and Music by JORGEN ELOFSSON,
MARTIN SANDBERG, PER MAGNUSSON
and DAVID KREUGER

YOU'LL BE IN MY HEART

(Pop Version)

from Walt Disney Pictures' TARZAN™

Words and Music by
PHIL COLLINS

Moderately

Come stop your cry - ing; it will be all right.

Just take my hand, hold it tight. I will pro - tect you from

all a - round you. I will be here; don't you cry.